W9-DEC-721

ALSO BY THE AUTHOR

Handwritten, Sun, 1979
Two Poems, Z Press, 1981
The Windows Flew Open, Burning Deck, 1991
Casting Sequences, University of Georgia Press, 1993
Signifying Art: Essays on Art After 1960, Cambridge University Press, 1999
Else, in Substance, Paradigm Press, 1999
The Annotated "Here" and Selected Poems, Coffee House Press, 2000
Begetting Textile, Equipage, 2000

ABOUT THE AUTHOR

Of the Diagram: The Work of Marjorie Welish, Slought Books, 2003

WORD GROUP

POEMS
BY
MARJORIE
WELISH

*For Chris Martin
on this historic occasion,
from Marjorie Welish
May 29, 2004*

COFFEE HOUSE PRESS

2004

Minneapolis

Coffee House Press books are available to the trade through our primary distributor, Consortium Book Sales & Distribution, 1045 Westgate Drive, St. Paul, MN 55114. For personal orders, catalogs, or other information, write to: Coffee House Press, 27 North Fourth Street, Suite 400, Minneapolis, MN 55401, www.coffeehousepress.org.

Coffee House Press is a nonprofit literary publishing house. Support from private foundations, corporate giving programs, government programs, and generous individuals help make the publication of our books possible. We gratefully acknowledge their support in detail in the back of this book.

ACKNOWLEDGMENTS

American Letters and Commentary: "Word and Object" • *Chicago Review:* "Seated Recklessly"
Conjunctions: "Delight Instruct" • *Facture:* "Clans, Moieties and Other"
Jacket [on-line]: "Weeping Branch" • *mark(s)* [on-line]: "Still Life with Witness"
The chapbook *Else, in Substance* is a publication of Paradigm Press (Providence, 1999). *Begetting Textile* is a chapbook written in partial fulfillment of a Howard Foundation Fellowship, published by Equipage (Cambridge, England, 2000). Journals having published these poems include: *American Poetry Review, The Gig* (Willowdale, Ontario), *How 2* [on-line], *Sulfur.*

"Deleting 'For Them This Brochure Is Unnecessary'" first appeared on-line through Philly Talks 19, Allan Fisher-Karen Mac Cormack (October 17, 2001), Slought Networks; written to *No. 1A*, 1948, by Jackson Pollock, formerly [untitled] now "1A" first appeared in *MOMA*, the magazine of The Museum of Modern Art, vol. 5 no.2, February 2002; "This Sort," "In the Name of Studio" and "Cities of the Table: Marginalia" originally written in honor of Burning Deck's fortieth anniversary; "Clams, Moieties and Other" together with "Cities of the Table" appear in full in *Of the Diagram: The Work of Marjorie Welish* by Slought Books, 2003.

After the on-line publication of "Cities of the Table: Marginalia" by Slought Networks, the sequence "Cities of the Table," in its entirety, appeared in *The Gig.* After appearing on-line through Slought Networks, the entirety of "In the Name of Studio" appeared in *Jubliat.*

Library of Congress Cataloging-in-Publication Data
Welish, Marjorie
Word group : poems / by Marjorie Welish.
p. cm.
ISBN 1-56689-157-4 (alk. paper)
I. Title.
PS3573.E4565W67 2004
811'.54—DC22   2004000676

FIRST EDITION | FIRST PRINTING
1 3 5 7 9 8 6 4 2
Printed in the United States

CONTENTS

I.

ELSE, IN SUBSTANCE

ELSE, IN SUBSTANCE

The dress
The other dress.

The recurrent dress
The perpetual dress.

The basic dress
The reductive dress.

The little dress
The little black dress.

The opaque dress
The remote dress.

The opaque dress
The mute dress.

Reply that
rhetorical dress

happens frequently
happens sufficiently

in explicit instances
in the works of X.

The dress.
The other dress.

The necessary dress
The contingent dress.

For the thesis that says
realizing the ideal

cannot be
in objects such as these

lexicons
not self-identical,

as of forgetful Greece,
say again,

say again,
in memoriam

happens always, frequently
in prophetic dress

of explicit instances:
Helen, merely a limiting case.

Missing mass [is] entailed dress
for the repudiating career.

The belletrist dress
The Situationist dress.

The meaningless dress
The meaninglessness of dress.

The dress, the other dress
propositional and repudiating

aftermath. Address
a blank space designating the loan

to a museum elsewhere
and the loan (plausibly) to here.

The dress in estimate
A dress explained.

The explained dresses, contemporary
The interpreted winter dress.

The dress
The idea of a dress.

Interpreting ware
Interpreting water.

Else, *in passim.*
Intuitions.

Either/or
and one eighth

without dress
throughout dress.

POSSIBLE FIRES

Constitutive of stone put down
grown by melting silt; artifice meets sourdough there; there deduced from fractured clay
matrix—and culture: culture's modern loaf induced. Let a leaf be cultural in this world;
then, let a leaf's waxy index of antihistamine eventually be an event it (the leaf) might not
have issued. Issue anything special. Anything medicinal, everything medicinal. Every-
thing medicinal and a breeze

pebbled with trial.
Over and under entities are a few pebbles, some trial and error.
The author has argued that error in Spain was commonplace.
Spain was a commonplace in Stein's alterity.
Stein featured Spain.
Down beneath the constructs, we tried "countenancing" a type;
here she tried automatism and "feature," in the sense of
        "structure, form or appearance esp. of a person":
a portrait void of appearance yet replete with animal gait.
A world with animals overlapped, with animals offset,
        offset in a sea change.

Everything medicinal and an afterthought—
but he had then to breathe
        giving cause
        creating occasion
intervening ambitiously in Spain's
reciprocating energies and commonplace.
Stein featured Spain
        as one featuring norms

as one featuring a build
   a build of beginnings
   a build of subroutine
with animals
  boar?
  pig?
offset in a sea change.

DETAINED BY REST

Detain nature in facsimile across nonchalance, against the grain. What is
an equivalent mat?

                Matter

translated and unlike, yet presumed in the phrase "our pro-foreignness"
or perhaps "aspirin." And "lyricism"

                                as cars

into carp. With carp permitted and speaking of impossibility, "soluble
fish," neither described nor defined stay far from comprehending white,
black, assiduously translating all this into a house, coincidently your havoc.

Do we require an ambulance? An ambulance to give a close reading and apply
instrumentality? Do you require sleep, do you require little sleep? They
lack sleep yet do not need it. They like entering into sincerity little
by little, toward subsidence. Under your very eyes is a little less rest.
Inhabitants detained by rest do not find sleep now, now lost

in cheap images. And entities move ordinarily fatigued, with
metal fatigue against iron, cast fatigue and sleep transpiring
a sentence notwithstanding plainness. Then there is less
fence in question.

                    Nettles are natural

reproof, properly of allergy (Helen had been deployed already). And ahead
travelers merge with stairs' rate of change.

                                On a list of things,

vagrants are decoded by mood, are decided by vagaries. Visitors enter the
Visitors' Entrance, also known as the Staff Entrance. At the border,
something points to its object: Bear right and take the lift to the fifth floor.
Follow the sign, indicating the way to the elevator; take it to the fifth floor.
Go right to the lift and press "5" for staff offices. A lift for all occasions
is somewhere positive in this facility, this district, these uphill areas.

                                                                    A change of

address: onto a fire escape in darkness, as a former architect,
for whom, like largesse over building, we are composing
translated fire escapes. The ones I have emphasized recant their

position, jet
West and East.

The politics of reading

have caught those moving stairs (as they were once called),
for epic purposes. In what sense are they then translations? In the climbing valley,
our gradual ascent, our newly incremental elevation ready-to-hand, escalators are
"redirected toward unprohibited objects." ("Faster," say the montagists.)
                                                                    Recite

something. Paraphrase a house or, in a phrase,

under deleterious influence, mentioning red, you pause at a district, I
forget the way back. The implausibility of translation confronts
the necessity of translation, commissioning descriptions of doing so. I forgot
the way back from scale to size. This is my portion.
                                                    Off these rocks,

sincerity did escort authenticity once; once, sincerity did shoulder
mountains in snow. Then later, literary torsos placed there cope with their being prior.
When you say "public," which public? When? Why? Or alternatively,

deputy literary criteria translate business listings into beauty: heavily again,
her own criteria list
                    lend
regularities
              stipulating this rock, these discursive rocks.

LESS MUSIC

This freedom up.
A house difficult of exit, diffident of exit.

This flame up.
The false house, house of faulty entries.

This facade up.
The manifold worries architecture.

This face up.
To the artifice's winding paths we lend our gloss.

This fact up!
This house multicursal and continuous.
Do you desire to disengage the frontispiece of devastating complexity?

This!
The curving house is green.
Do you wish to disappear from an escaping sentence?

Do you wish to forget the manuscript or do you wish to evict the manuscript?
This froth up.
The house ancient of exit, of antecedent impressions.

THE LOGICS

Up side this!
This me up
for a little grammar
for grammar not minute

but prefigured
near deities
on the same level
maintaining level.

The logics of plus and minus.
The logic of love is mirage; later, editorial glosses.
Love's ratio tantalizes.
Analytic love is exceptional.
After longing, love leaves a trail of imperatives.
The logistics of allurement are nearly endless.
Fastening and unfastening logic is love in love.
The logics that obtain in fascination.
In love, fastening and unfastening logic.
A fraction of love fascinates.
Logic through lyric is, arguably, intriguing,
and a lure for more of it.

The logic of love is fascination: by which is meant or may be meant
that logic in love is operative word-for-word yet in no direct equivalent
for the other regard unlike yet closer (or close as a likeness)
in register. *Arte povera* and flutes not mentioned—an archaicism surviving.

So, too, the schemata of your imaginary: "Have you ever been in love?"
"No, but I've been in like." By which judicious logic is love in aesthetic
detachment from estimates and etcetera such that analytic
hypotheses are there to substitute for worlds that tell us nothing. "The,"
for "a," in some poetics. Is fascination retrograde? Retrograde etching
from within sentiment and lagging, love in love with logic and the horizon
of the ozone, by which one of us is everything and the other, everything;
and we loved the logic two, three, and many fast trials. The logic held
and we were fascinated, slow in our experiments. Unextinguished
monochromes would be instances of assigning touch.

Do you want to escape without saving this page?
Do you want to escape only to retrieve triumphant negation?
Do you want to escape affirmation, wreak havoc on the positive data?
Do you wish to escape sense?
Do you wish to discredit the page?
Do you wish to restore the page to grace?
Do you allege foreshortening matter?
Do you want to escape favorite pages, passages, and awake?
Do you regret this page, that is, its usurpation through textual advances?
Do you wish to make amends?
Do you wish to mend the erasure?
Do you want to illuminate the erasure?
Do you want to leave without defining a page?
Do you want to leave with anything whatsoever?
Do you want to eject from the program without escaping confinement?
Do you want to defend the attempt?
Do you want to escape the attempt without acknowledgment?

Let us consider the house difficult of exit. Regarded as given
is ingenuity. Walls would differ for every subject. Clocks anachronistic

and/or historical and unquestionable portrayals of yourself in convex
oculi of water—no, the walls in diaspora have yielded to reflection
in which is pictured a defunct inhabitant idealized and very near, much
more large for being prudent from high up to fulfill the office, long,
long ago—simulacra in voices having succumbed to the last of the epitaphs
and the corners have fallen into oblivion, fallen out of favor yet
revealing a mental faculty on the obverse screens on which interior
fictions on canvas are unfolding and otherwise epitomize textual
corrective (quite a riot of practice) from dawn to dusk and here to
eternity, in engravings actually given him by the aged Piranesi, a profile
of nothingness mathematically, yet given to marshaling smallness, the
formulation extends some aims of the architect upward and downward to a
curio underground reflecting morbidity and its variants. Low ceilings,
tessellated logic, and stale visual jokes "peep around corners" in the
grotto giving way to an encyclopedia of casts. Cast encyclopedia pages
isolating study through type and types giving in to the occasional
specificity—"Because they are best when they're soonest put out!"—effect
of remote cause and logic, toward the floor above us low enough to put a
ceiling within reach, reflecting underground sensibilities, down and out
sky "from nowhere" aims an architecture outside in, inside out and
formulated, yet because of its relative smallness, a profile illustrative of
eternity engraved in dusk and otherwise epitomizing textual corrective.
"What do you see here?" "Historicism! Historicism's primal scene,"
surprised you did not know text when you see it unfolding fictions
reversible to exterior projections fallen out of favor. And the corners
having succumbed to watery antechambers long ago . . .

FALSE ENTRY

"When is a door not a door?"

"Sometimes black, sometimes white, I have veins but no blood!"

"There is a red lady locked up in a room whose door is often open yet
  she can never escape."

"There are two splendid horses, one black as pitch, one as of crystal; each runs ahead
  of the other but can never catch or seize it."

Two cars approach an intersection. Which has the right-of-way?

What are the hand signals for a stop? For a right turn?

In which situations may you pass a vehicle to the right?

Having completed a left turn from a two-way onto the one-way street, where
  should your car be, in what lane?

"What is green on the mountain, black in the marketplace, and red in the house?"

"What is black and white and red all over?"

"In the fields grazes a calf whose body does change thrice in the space of a day:
  first white, then red, then black at last."

"There is an enclosure with ten doors: when one is open, nine are shut; when nine
  are open, one is shut."

THE GLOVE

"Always in face, never in fact."
"Always in house, never at home."
"Always leaves a glove longer."
"A horse walks into a bar . . . " where are we now?

". . . a thousand lights in a dish."
". . . comes and goes and leaves a white glove
      at the window."
"How do you make a road broad?"
"A horse walks into a bar."

Once a blue glove folded like this
      like this bronze.
Once a fire unabridged if underweight
      scraped paint away.
Once a face set axes upon which
      hung paradoxes.
"A horse walks into a bar."

"Where once the id, now the ego."
"I, too, once knew Arcadia."
"A horse walks into a bar."
"Once upon a time," alleged.

II.

BEGETTING TEXTILE

TEXTILE 1

As if
    "And somewhere other than observable water"

Insofar as
        surfeits
            "and the separation may possess its own corrective"

or domino.
      "What the lyric can comprehend"
                    in many-valued trespass

as soon as
      trellis in everything.

Pallor won.
      To attain to urban corrective
              another symposium

advocating a long escarpment
          of references
             a convection current

not floral
      but what the lyric can comprehend
              "wetting her skirt."

Insofar as

assets

drying his shirt

lyrically, faithfully floral

up to and including incomprehension

convection

advocating little posits, immense thickness.

Of references,

we prefer all threads.

Seething

the self-same traffic.

Symposia attain to because,

because

gymnasia attain to

a planet.

Crushed colors

"Two lacks."

TEXTILE 2

As if
      answerable to anthem
                      in antis

Even as

Insofar as

as
    as illustrated
           As illustrated milk

spilt on printers' ink, throughout protest movement
                                sparkling

rhetoric!

As
    meaning for the reason that

because a

because a
      caustic cure
           of or relating to the Caucasus.

As if

    The envelope of rays

Insofar as

    "the envelope of rays emanating from a point"

Even as

    "the envelope of rays emanating from a point and reflected or refracted by curved

surfaces"

    and cottage curtains.

        Unhomeliness.

TEXTILE 3

As if
    exhausting sunset
        alongside them

Even as
    inexhaustible sunset
        throughout us

Insofar as
    already given in exhaust
        carried over

as the portrait
    which is to say the perceptual prototype.
        "Perhaps he meant postcard-like."

As illustrated
    the vulgate in the landscape, the landscape prospect
        at the poem's close.

"Let me finish"
    light density,
        an introduction.

TEXTILE 4

As if
> choosing exhaustiveness
>> on wood

Because
> breathing exhaustiveness in substance not completeness
>> struck paper

As if
> exhausting universities
>> with haze

As
> exhausting universities exhaust their patrimony
>> in wax

Insofar as
> else, in substance is
>> iron in scarce wax

Because
> not else in essence, rather anything.
>> "Metal," she heard.

Because

      not anything, something

             metal: iron, I think.

As

     specific person in generic song,

             "That's me, in hardware"

insofar as

      a person is gesticulating at a thing through a thing thing

even as

      quiddities in pictures tangled.

TEXTILE 5

As if,
      then.
            Such is not always the case

because
        allegations and tougher
                units

of corresponding bias
            and a vivacious clipping service
                    flash,

or for the reason that
          literature conjectures across texts
                  and carcass

with reading.
        For what reason?

For the reason that
          a further allegation can provide
                  qualms

as
    intertext,
        three decades of

sand

    as if shadow.

        Shadow

as if sand

    meddled with windshield.

        A further comfort

insofar as

    the forward edge of reading

        made material conjecture.

As if

    conjecture is international: a vivacious clipping service

        and a species of

pavilion.

    For what reading?

        "Pavilion, your rooms are coming down!"

TEXTILE 6

Insofar as

    the turnstile within sentences attributed spaces

        like illness across thick lulls

and insofar as

    sentences apparently exact hard spaces, posthumous definitions,

deficits

    auxiliary surfaces in our reading also.

        "The rush of pealing bells cries out in the gorges"

has forwarded how things might have been different.

        A different thing.

TEXTILE 7

And as in the mind

        a gyroscope

            through and beyond gossip

"Of what is past, or passing, or to come"

            and its corollaries.

                And its copyright

as in the estate of "Gates of Hell"

            cooling off

              original copies.

As posthumous descriptions

           the body in dark and light descant

                wax met metal

and lost. As he left them as he let them go:

           ash let bodies be copied cordially.

                "We've met before."

We have lived in emphasis

           to establish the mettle of nature

              for somewhere

literary entities have disembarked.

           "Landscapes," they are called.

              Culled

because on land

        —"That's not a garden, that's a sanatorium for plants"—,

                              a sanatorium for flora

in attendance

        has found its women's literature.

                  False positives

". . . as a late cultural arrival . . ."

            as, for example, locale

                  or tanning

even as a reticent reader works through such maneuvers.

TEXTILE 8

As posthumous
        description "Of what is past, or passing . . ."
                              past perfect
in attendance, dancer from dance:
                   we are its offshoot
                        almost

thoroughly passage throughout passing face;
                    step-down
                      with steep

passion at the summit, the summary.
                Similar kinds are common
                        common

and demonstrably cultural at the close of the poem

whereas
        in the beginning was a natural reference table
                      my table

interpenetrating vocabularies
              winged embroideries
                  episodes

of nature and culture varying inversely in verse

                    in bas-relief

                        in relief

as of

    aged phrase; add new rhetoric beneath

                add great

settlement "From Abstraction to Design Argument"

                    supplement

                      subscript

even as

    ear to glacier, glassware give and take, deal justly.

                  Or adjust

"sheen"

    (in the sense of "pretext")

            or make sense of . . .

explicit destination and planet, lanes

          passing lanes closely annexed;

                  annex

prompting lanes

    lanes with the propensity for assent

            promised ascent.

TEXTILE 9

"you refuse to become a deer or a tree"

Pictorial, if contemporary—no, contemporarily:

We

a deer again.

Is contemporary art modern?

She

as girl inhabited, inhabiting thirsty house, Louise—

"an iconographic setback."

You

This dark tree improvising

pictorialism: how many faces can you find?

He

A form of because

finding faces is explanatory, *malheureusement.*

We

a form of because

in surface

causing

a white wall as an effect of modernity at midnight.

Plane

formulates because

        insofar as hunting has brought a buck into meter, the hunter's meter.

                        Reflective surface

insofar as

       the silhouetted tree is a semblance: silhouetted tree, a semblance

                    of an aspect

of Goethe.

      Of Goethe arborescent, in an aspect of being afflicted

                surface

a surfeit of aspect, affect

       of Goethe as textual; more text than house, housed.

                   Point

as a net: they have netted themselves

        a form of because in pointing to it.

                 Point to it.

Being chased.

     Directly to poetics.

        A slice.

TEXTILE 10

A jumper knitted throughout, a sweater's overcoming mimesis

Less

"Chapter 1 has been suspended in a warehouse / of textiles for 1000th of a second"—at once a sentence and a sentence in a poetics.

Lesser

at once a linguistic event and a linguistic event styled after installation.

Least

Impossible work finds hypothetical situations.

Good

Situations impersonating a book, speech acts walking across stage

Better

situations impersonating a boot, speech acts walking across a stag.

Best

Suspended in a warehouse, a literacy campaign

Loudest

suspended in a disused textile factory, textiles and a second literacy campaign after cultural evisceration.

Louder

A woman removing her jumper (sweater) in a textile factory

Loud

removes a jumper (sweater), then another pulled inside out, says aloud, "And now, for the retrograde inversion."

TEXTILE II

Because, then

        if, then, then even as

                such as in voice-over

"'because,' Schubert writes . . ."

    "'Nevertheless, your life / seems to me wide with potential because of your /. . .'"

"because" pageant:

          to give voice to a cause

                choir

to ascertain causes beyond rhetoric

              chorus.

Causality in lyric is trying.

          A song, a song beyond rhetoric

                    ours

insofar as . . .

      let us each in turn declare

causes

    the disenchantment to which we write cheques

"Nevertheless, your life / seems to me wide with potential because of your /

                                                                        modesty."

                                                                A vocal

"'because,' Schubert writes"

                        a voiceprint

"'as if,' Franz Schubert writes"

                        I am here

"because" pageant in the twentieth century.

                                A path limited

                                                mitered, yet a path

because, in the sense of

                "That I am here"

                                Encore

or to give voice to a cause beyond rhetoric.

                                Let us each voice

                                                (the vocals of . . .)

the causes to which we do in fact write cheques.

                                (Tell 'em, Ella.)

TEXTILE 12

A path formatted. A chapter.

> "There cannot be a chapter formatted differently,"

she said, "like a sore thumb."

> "A chapter formatted differently from these is not a sore thumb,"

I said, "but an opposable thumb, an opposable thumb with its own instrumentality."

> A train

"... hear that train strumming ..."

> "without the doubt of a shadow"

Agora shadowless and "shadowless"

> path.

Which?

> "In recent years he has researched the share"

a path formatted across a wave.

> There cannot be a wave formatted otherwise

she said, like a wheel.

> A wave in syntax such as that is no sore wheel,

I said, but a solemn wheel (no one-sided wheel, I said, a level) with its own instrumentality.

A door

"folded like a sheet of paper . . ."

"You were the most beautiful of them all."

"Now I begin to paint shadows in."

Out-of-print—

which?

In recent years he has researched the interval

which?

In recent years he has researched the inconvenience

a path formatted across hot water.

There cannot be hot water formatted symptomatically,

she said, like fumes.

TEXTILE 13

Locomotive

What is a portrait?

Locomotive

When is a portrait not a portrait?

When it is locomotive

not physiognomic

insofar as pasturing.

"Tendency of ideas to go over into movement"

Movement

as such.

Movement was used.

Walking along a walk

"as fully as possible."

Walking the walk

Stance? Pavement?

As passage.

As passage to pavement

walking the walk

republished as

"Tendency of ideas to go over into movement.

For these experiments

the subject was given a pencil."

By the people.

Men At Work.

As in the phrase

"working women."

TEXTILE 14

Because the sighted believe themselves to be visually literate . . .

because we who are sighted underneath do not believe their literary

sentence: the social process of a huge mallet

predicated on identifying pink
                          Pollock or not
                                    —hot—

with decor with mentions

designated areas of mention

whatever the language however the language why . . .

beneath the language however through language: why
                                              subtext
                                                —sum—

cut corners

cut-and-dried

"without the terms *picare* and *explicare*

used to indicate respectively: the act of rolling and unrolling"

Because sequence is the pilot driven to commitment

because sequence is not automatic pilot but story committed

                                                           a rhetoric

                                                                 —hot—

as much as a set of descriptive comings and goings

as much as anticipated comings and goings

                                     handsomer by half

                                                —sum.

Because if basic then pink, if pink then sissy—no,

savvy because if pink then chrome made

                                    intelligible field:

                                              Spill—

automotive cocktail automotive taillights

auto cocktail automotive taillights

                                    electric

                             —bulk.

Because mathematical, electrifying entities construct us squinting

because mathematically electrifying pilots construct
                                             persiflage in poets,
                                                       spill

I say: Does it matter if you're *wrong?* Then I say

Does it matter that which disproves you? Then you say
                                   Matter.
                                        Bulk.

Which is a coincidence: ". . . itself must, at all points, be a high-energy construct . . ."

Which is fusion itself: at points, be a high-energy construct
                                        or else
                                             —spill.
                    [alternative ending]   —The Atlantic.

TEXTILE 15

The barge placed heavily into water the fast demise

in performances by that heavy barge bearing alphabet
                                        —"The flood receding, they returned"—
placed into attractive water heavily. Surprise

crowdedness of the throat with a better
                                        —"The pages deleted, they returned"—

unwatched art and literature on the barge heavily in the basin

literature sinking water impersonating the fast moving words
                                        —Rain suited to tape—

displacing the voice something there like butterflies and the democratic

"Cement," an ancient song a song without words
                                        —Poise suited to tape—

motoring the voice through the water heavily and fast

with encyclopedic capacity yet condensing "Atlantic Cement"
                                        —"but those sounds make sense to me"—

or should happen as a body "Atlantic Cement" in performance

perforating water over water making time longer and lower

—"Abide with me"—

against the trajectory indicated. Encyclopedic capacity with a compass

nose unwatched the barge attractive to water and mortar

—"mortality / weighs heavily"—

is active in displacing water for the blunt yet fast appearance

of The Atlantic in literature on which "Atlantic" is a surface so

—"an accidental double exposure, apparently"—

reflecting that encyclopedia cemented with capacity

except the capacity for comprehension. Motoring so

with attractive water large blocks indicating next

element or entity or item move fast if heavily.

TEXTILE 16

For the reason that "and repeats and repeats in my ear"

"Reading where I have written"

even as "reading where I have written"

may have written, shall have

stencils

insofar as the new rhetoric

We reap before a single hearer

everything in motion, nothing in motion

as argumentation

and as argumentation, she motioned us to come forward

nails in hand

because action is necessary.

Two women within earshot:

arranged chronologically

even as cross-referenced

referring in mention, not without

skills

such as these and as these

"Two women within earshot

        proximate

as argumentation

        and as argumentation, one says

                'Fine snap

peas,'

        And as argumentation, the other says 'Yes,

                the old skills are coming back.'"

as "rowing side by side"

        is written as argumentation by him on a ream.

                Of obstacles

as minimal, anti-form, systems.

III.

WORD GROUP

THE SIGNAGE THAT WAS THERE

Are all contingencies still in effect? Okay, okay, okay.
A sensible object rules the etcher. As if for you.
As for the sensible object without rules, phrases
writing to dedicate what, how and why
in sentences they say that they say they say:
what *ad infinitum* is it?

They say that they say that they say the word "light"
having caressed a sensible object and other still gluey
led moths to fatigue. They say that they say that fermenting
aftermaths, not having the same obscure fatigue, quite believe you;
few are those who understand the scope of your convalescence,
the seascape of your convalescence.

X pauses. Y pauses and turns, runs.
Z pauses, turns and catches the incandescent
sentence in seascape, having caressed
an obscure fatigue or retreat from the sensible object.
That's a replica. That's a cautious wavelet
always, sometimes . . .

A few aftermaths are always already in transit,
obscure yet transverse as though to emit
the past or the past now
excavated and left methodically, if partially,
translated attention to which he dedicates this detritus:
we met, it melted, it melted infinitesimal hazard
courtesy of comings and goings.

Not now left and once since left, let alone
in an unemphatic state are a few aftermaths—this,
an unpresentable translation from English
as a possible index of streaming incommensurables. Okay, okay.
An upsurge of slurred speech
dedicates itself to unpresentable detritus
"we would still have to detail" re an anterior future.

I shall be with you momentarily.
"See you later," expresses all of an impressive
soon. Of what will have been done,
met, melted. The detritus
of or relating to all or some or none, From . . . To . . . as possibly okay
infill and efficacy expresses an impressive waste:

as soon as they leave, insofar as
they will have left, been apart from
and left alone as remainder, not sentence,
occupied the aftermaths
entered. Exit. "Where's the exit?"
"See you later" sent for
slurred speech adapted to the art of inscription.

We tripped up on all aftermaths but one.
I shall be with you momentarily.
One moment, please!
Are all remote? "It melted"—a rude text
left in the wake of retreat like some maths.
In Scotland reverting to speech was a sign of self-rule—
"I like the idea."

What is it? "Our expectation that 'it' will continue."

"That's something," we rewrote.

My name is . . . What time do you close?

Can you show me on the map? "My name is . . . ," she continues.

THIS SORT

1.

In a plane, plot, or gravitational pull, negative or interrogative.
Glosses

          Without pronouncing it

The zone in sum

        gravitational accident

gravitational microphones

2.

Histories of the subjugated read as serious scatter

                              vernaculars

        smote by a microchip

"And he does so."

3.

His effort to talk

        through and through

WORD AND OBJECT

Assigning probabilities to fluid
surfaces or spectacular approximations
in a departed *polis*
    ("I'm empathizing with Christmas trees; I must be mildly depressed.")
and in responding to modernity once again, much interim
    (Scandinavian installations of dead and dying evergreens)
permits a signature postmodernity, and smears "Is the same with itself"
    (reinventing a rented nomenclature)
through arts and letters. Looking up from underneath . . .

Glass, not my field, shelves of it nonetheless and at eye level
a glacier transparent, translucent and opaque
such that complementaries were visible
synthesized of "stimulating negation"
and experienced in seizing a shard of front and back
facets together: Goethe through apparition
    (ever yellow over blue).

Ever over ever oval ever aorta
of electric dress—painted light bulbs, electric cords, and timer—
intra-sentence attempts the ultimate sacrilege.
They are empathizing with straw
and confusing it with aesthetic
inventories
    ("Green," meaning "unseasoned")
They are empathetic straw, empathetic north
and faltering narrative

which is vibrating sympathetically with a past
path and likenesses
        (in young greens, aromatic)

lyrical subdivisions neither here nor there
        (here and there, and there and)
a fragment of half, and half through half-hearted aorta
in intensive care. In intensive care, he opened his eyes
to say, "I'm sorry." Electric cords and timer and painted bulbs
cascading over her—a piece created to be cast

glass, not my field. The clarity of the lack
seizing eye level provides a companion
to epistemology in the description where it folds back.
We live in a harrowing relativism
of hue flaring into value. Apprehended when spreading
        (ever rain green bow rain bow ever card
         ever green ever ready ever view green ever
         green card ever green re view life jacket).

Glass and transparent blind
spot—"he had repeated the epithet 'beautiful' a hundred times"—yet
to the left or right an instrumentality and vase synthesized;
seizing front widespread blind only for regarding spot beyond
yet through, an outbreak of value at eye level apprehended
in the beaker showing rainbow as we walked wearing our clothing.

The class of things evacuated in the center, transparently then opaquely.

CLANS, MOIETIES AND OTHER

Used and out-of-print books classified as steppe. Fish were an important supplement.
Only printed words. Forty-two children's . . . Territory there in the archive frequents
    an inkling
or inking: Eskimo, harpoon, seal; Australian aborigine, boomerang, kangaroo—
    throughout
image, music, text. After a few uniformities, traps and axes acquire traits of
    amphitheaters and tribunes.

Where is the true red, yellow, or blue? is wearing a stubbornness in which two reds,
    two yellows,
two blues, vie for that distinction. Who's Afraid of Nouns, Verbs, and Adjectives?
Band exogamy: in exchange, hunting, dancing, gambling. Whereabouts of the winter
    encampment,
whereabouts of less strongly tied margins of error. A fish weir similar to ours.

Where red, yellow, and blue is a commonplace diving under yellow in some scheme of
    left and right counter
tops, to be sent up to be as sky to the earth's black and white, ivory black and/or lamp
    black. Lamp and
mirror shade to keep away composure: blues will do it, as will jazz blues,
Orpheus! The deceased were burned and buried, or bound and buried, the former in
    the low lands.

Baseball. Prehistoric football, AND, OR, BUT NOT unlike surpluses.

IA

Or as if a writ sputtered white noise in a blackout and slammed wiring
into a sink to sink a sink in a blackout bitter white: text that was once the writ
might have been vapor; a script sinking the scratch sinking throughout

and/or throughout hypothetically saying "salt" through noise hypothetically
even as white noise vaporizes tar scratched (not from the wrist, from the ambit
of an aqua duct) insofar as saying, insofar as inscribed as if where

splashed salt; splashed salt across noise from the ambit of
saying something thoroughly although as if the hand might have said it
memoranda were sputtered as the—even as the inscription itself

appears to be that of a participle wringing-wet is such that this
acquaints the script of which edit or intro an "as if"
is that of the crush the crushed surrogate saying something—some with

and the rest of it—extremely broad pinpointing and insofar as wiring
the ambit of memoranda (not from the wrist, from the shoulder)
inscription itself: a scratch across an aqua duct even as white noise

hypothetically because, the splash of a scratch sacrificed from a wrist
of hydraulic mental representations vaporized which we wrote
as if saying "What?" The without of "as if" wringing-wet until now.

STILL LIFE WITH WITNESS

1.
Q. Why paint?
A. Why write?

A scanned version of your pen-and-ink signature ran late.
Why, then, have you not forsworn writing altogether
Frame: technology

altogether signature with pen to paper;
have you forsworn reading as well
Frame: culture

and/or altogether to textual implementation with/without
talk/not talking the laws of and/or the way out
Frame: logic

work, the work of thought, selected and pivotal
which is to say definitive or failing that
Frame: theory

pursuit strikingly tolerant
if not philanthropic
Frame: value

". . . by failing to define exactly what a signature is"
". . . by failing to define what a signature is"?
  Frame: law

2.

Q. Why paint?

A. Why write?

Why then have you not forsworn writing implements as such, weights and measures if
    not wrought iron

Frame: technology

altogether signature written with pen to paper and cursive drapery "prepared to handle
    underestimation"?

Frame: index

Why have you not shunned writing altogether, abstract/concrete implementation
    with/without horizontals odd/even reentry into alphabet?

Frame: logic

Why have you not gone on a fast for writing and difference, atoning for work, the work
    of thought, selected and pivotal

Frame: economy

writing, if not philanthropic, then serrated: an interview left unedited to fix a likeness;
    edited, the interviews retrieved from a competing archive

Frame: value

"by failing to define exactly what a signature is" in digital epochs, somnolent in not
    having written legislation?

Frame: law

WORD GROUP

"I" investigate
"I" sing
 itinerary

 modern American usage
 a writer's guide to copyright
 a manual of style

 signifying art
"I" may investigate
"I" might have sung

 a writer's guide
 and furthermore
 a branch

 of freeze frames
 the art of
"We"

"We" in speech; "I" across song
 violated in this meadow of
"we," a branch

 of Eisenstein
 to show that "we" sing against which
"I" speak, leaning against

silence. The sudden deposit
of boy
in the arms. Deposit the boy.

That is, the sudden deposit
of boy against opening iris
to show that ebb,

to show that ebb augmented,
augmenting dawn through a lexicon
of profanity, in intellectual

property, a writer's guide.

Our signature
investigated
his dissertation,

an impenetrable writer's guide
or incitement, and furthermore,
a branch, a blossoming branch close up

in tributaries. Vivid stills
improve the edition.
"We," an everyman

in tableaux. Stop.
"We" speak. Stop.
"I" sing. Stop.

"We," a blossoming branch
  against which meadow
"I" speak, seriously rent

  shot numb for that residuum
  of ideology, as for that shot
  delighted with it, retentive

  ignited. Freeze frames radiant:
  "Freeze!" he shouted abundantly
  in ideological ice.

  Ideology, be still.
  Lo! Tableaux vivants.
  Look! Vivid arrest!

WEEPING BRANCH

1.
Mist in modern discourse
protesting decor, *Lavender Mist*.

Dismissive of mist's specifications
and spacing on canvas, you now have

know-how—decorative, unless it is axiomatic
lyricism; the lyric,

not too decorative, unless it is
complacent. Prejudicial against lyric

when he said too decorative,
and so-so. Begetting

a folio.
No synonymy here.

You and your crazy appetite
for pink, embracing the entire antipathy

and craze. Pink and black automotive
rhetoric, half camp/half criticism, fuchsia

usage arousing fear with precisely arborescent
irony toward consensus, which does undo, leaps out at the reader.

Decor if and only if complacent pastel.
The world is made up of brains in vats.

The world is a boat.
The world is dated half-truth:

1200, the author says 1950: which
something: epical, lyrical, epical-lyrical,

dramatic—which omitted category
is it?: 1968; yes, but which 1968?: 1789 or 1815;

1855 or 1890 or 1913 or 1948?
Now we are of the belief

there is an epistemology for all occasions,
systemic black and silver, silver and error.

Satyric pink and black proclaimed again
face to face, and on the mouth.

2.
An answer obscuring lyricism, the lyric
the lyre

in radio waves. Prejudicial against
the lyric, he bruised it,

then he took it from a confusion
of lyricism and lyric

and the calligram. Dissent and enterprising
letters so begetting a folio: the lyric.

You and your crazy cocktails, pink and black,
lyric silvered

and *Four Saints*, revealing her period
lyricism.

SEATED RECKLESSLY

I

1.

Modernity recto and verso
(Faust sits restlessly at his desk, in his armchairs)

2.

Pencil to paper automotively
ceding to a curious mesmerism
in her method, some self-medicating
sets of assumptions
occluding that
modernism free from Victorian
techno-poetics
(At his desk, his arms, Faust)
the techno-poetic occult. The
murmur . . .
(At his desk, Faust sits in his arms)
The dog ran, circling that occult
by means of his senses
probably not occult, only training
and/or translated dog.

(In a high-vaulted Gothic room, Faust, seated restlessly)
Less likely through spirit than through how taught.
My little dog knows—in what sense?

3.

(In a high-vaulted chair in his only room, Faust sits)
Sitting—in what sense? With what faculty?
Differing to affirm that modernity—
Dust on a Kosovar doll, "You can't buy it,
you can't sell it, you can't give it away"—
sheltering alternative poetry
to that which finds no value in dust,

we may dispute
that the automobile is indexical of a public
in a public life—"I am afraid
to be rich in America," the Kosovar said.

II

1.

Modernity in calendar and orthography
(Faust in eclipse)

2.

Sunday for today and today only
a news pad, a newspaper
through paste has occluded that
edit, in favor of sleight-of-hand
leap: through darkroom
(Faust, head in hands)
the lost darkroom,
the performed darkroom
(The valise of hands, his)
even as an orbiting dog

traces an odor
as though through a diurnal
begetting, set and reset
(*At the high, vaulted desk, Faust sits, head in hands*)
in a likeness of sorts.
My little dog in heaven and on earth.

3.
(*Desk, minus Faust*)
At rest—in what sense? With what faculty
doubling to apply maximally
to sentences and their surfaces.
No dust here, where the ball
slaps a penny between us. Take a step
in sheltering alternative poetry, although why

Stein's possessing an auto
should be thought to be public
writing throws scripted shadows.

III
1.
Modernity's slip case
(*Faust may or may not be on the approach*)

2.
Paste to paper, paper to paste
in a method curiously mesmerizing
grammar and its sources
in torn paper writ large
occluding that

edit, itself a convoy

of techno-poetics

(Faust has opened the box, is about to open it)

duplicated. The

thickness . . .

(Faust has approached the indecipherable box)

A dog has drawn circles bodily:

from nose to tail is instinctual

and/or coincident

in likelihood.

(Within a high-vaulted box, Faust sits restlessly)

In all likelihood a coincidence

as in the expression of "following his nose"

in the sense of "by instinct," the dog senses such and such.

3.

(At a box he perhaps has opened, Faust sits)

Seance—in what sense? With what faculty?

Modernity raised on posts differentiates moods and tenses,

a modicum of reduction differentiates use

from dust and flakes cordial to picture books

for Russian children: children's things

sheltering alternative poetry:

hunter hunts hunted.

Who hunts? What does the hunter hunt?

With what implement? With what implement

indexical of a public life will have been started

by now? Startled by now? A book started.

BALLET AT CROSSWALK

He will have done so in recent lists advancing on the table.
Is the foreshortened table subtracting format? Let go!
Our lost object is not "I apologize."
We take for granted "17. A sequel to 12. A harmony"
swallowed poetics. Insert water
table—its stencils, at least, prophetic insofar as these
advance a slate. Walk. Run. *Fielding Sixes,*
Inlets, Pictures redistribute the paragraphs. Is the table there?
The table is here. Where are the instantly sliding doors?
Restating insinuated adventure for the torso
ought to be between. What is the schedule for *Torse?*
Ought/ought not "shines in our glasses." Or to restart our glass:
a deceptive simplicity
likes you, the attribution of shadow afterward:
it is raining. Start here! Have we met?
Chairs without backs. Admitting the redistribution
of dragged idiolects meant not an eccentricity
for marionettes but a table of contents
with respect to it. It? Them? Pagination
need not detain us. The soluble entity is on the table,
the sedimented table. "Stand roughly there" now voices
areas and informality in the floor plan,
the breathing floor plan? The plane of the floor
meets the plane of the table in this objective.
He choreographed for "roughly there."

A POPULACE

1.

One, setting Mayakovsky to doggerel gait,
another, banishing Mayakovsky to verse,
oblivious to literariness, spat out.

2.

"Two is profound ignorance," he said.
"To mention the ideology is to dis the poetics," I said.
"Two, to, and too," they said, while she said, "Three in a tram believe

3.

apparatus that is there, here and current
in a running jump, postulating a visit to the running board."

4.

"To propose the poetics of the running jump," he said,
"less to the risk of finding that this shadow, this second shadow, this third shadow, . . ."

5.

I catch my balance, waving terribly.
And again / the walls of the burning steppe / ring and sigh in the ear with the two-step.

All smokers / always and everywhere prefer . . .

MAQUETTE FOR AN ADVERTISEMENT

"Maquette for an advertisement for Krasnaia Zvezda (Red Star) cigarettes, 1923.
Gouache on paper, 8 15/16" x 17 5/8" (22.7 x 44.8 cm).
Text by Vladimir Mayakovsky.
Howard Schickler Fine Art, New York."

This third shadow there that gripped here toward which the straw bent
text—I am thinking not of Mayakovsky but of how shortcomings came to be bent
in subjugated countries: Maquette for Crisis.

To the question, "What is Mayakovsky's status in Poland today?"
he said, "I think . . .
I think 'avant-garde' does not apply," he said.
"I am thinking of how to explain . . . ," and (like Fassbinder)
investigate, critically. His own position.
To the avant-garde in Poland today, he set the question.
He sent a questionnaire.
"That is a very good question," he said slowly.
To the question, "What is Mayakovsky's status in Poland today?" said lengthily, rapidly,
said rapidly with regard to poetry.
Said Andante.
Composed of folded sheets.
"That is a printed situation," he said.
Said the question, "In what esteem does Poland hold his poetry, his poetics?"
Came the reply, "I myself wondered this."

DELETING "FOR THEM THIS BROCHURE IS UNNECESSARY"

1.

Sequences implicate sets corresponding. Contemporary societies . . .
we at once began; the future will likely consum-
tion of a representation. Anyone else, anyone else's litter
making literal his "tion" of a representation to impregnate
blue and green matches (after hav- —after that date, never—
ing its tides). From the left, a predicate out of breath
delays category, and sometimes not.
Histories of the subjugated read otherwise
than do those of the victorious.

                              And rising is 1913, almost always
being coextensive with 1690, the 9th century pending and within sight of
an inch of water in a basin. Minutes in a neolithic settlement.

2.

We at once began corresponding; the future will likely strip-search, will likely anthol-
tion of a representation. Anyone else, anyone else's litter, the book's first half
making literal his "tion" of sonorous velocities permeated and said,
unfailingly blue from green, origin of (after hav- —after that date, never—
ing its tides). From the left, a predicate short of breath, the hand lifted
"skeptical" and "agora" together, and sometimes not.
Histories of the subjugated read other's dicta
than do those of the victorious.

                              Your uppermost story is 1913
much of the time eclipsed in 1690, the 9th century pending . . . and felt it
writing in a basin. Minutes adapted to a neolithic settlement.

3.

tion of a representation. Anyone else, anyone else's litter
making literal his lay launderette for "tion" of "imitation" to impregnate
ultramarine and/or cobalt (after hav- —after that date, never—
ing its tides). "Prefabricated wiring with insulation and terminals" left a predicate breathless,
territory together with category transposed sometimes, as
histories of the subjugated read edgewise and are dusty, other
than those of the victorious.
                              Uppermost is 1913, immense, simultaneously
being read with 1690; the 9th century took place within sight of
an inch of anathema. Minutes passed a neolithic settlement.

4.

making literal his "tion" of "imitation" to impregnate
two blues: scarcely red, in being green (after hav- —after that date, never—
ing its tides). From stage left and clockwise, what is said of a fan
ventilating category, quantity and number, and sometimes
histories of the subjugated reverse. Speak through it, thickening. If you . . .
than do those of the victorious.
                              Theory of 1913 is as a fresh start, and uppermost is
your being multi-linear. In 1690, the 9th century took place and caused/was caused by
an inch of anathema, the basin as such, a split-second neolithic settlement.

5.

blue and green aspects (after hav- —after that date, never—
ing its tides). From the left wing, a predicate retaliated and walked out,
territory rewritten in category, and sometimes
histories of the subjugated read as vernacular
underestimated, its entablature
reserved to describe a serious scatter of tubing above a disposition.

                                        Particles of 1913,

teenth century being read with 1690; the 9th century will burst
an inch of a thing done. Day passed a neolithic settlement.

IV.

IN THE NAME OF STUDIO

IN THE NAME OF STUDIO

for Norma Cole

A STUDIO

Cadmium Yellow Lemon
Cadmium Yellow Light

STUDIO: 1994

Cadmium Yellow Lemon
Cadmium Yellow Light,
and the eye of a blackbird.

Paper halved to indicate
that Cadmium Yellow Light
is not Cadmium Yellow Lemon.

Throughout atrium
Cadmium Yellow Light
acquiring ground and air.

Left and right brilliant
if unintelligible yellow and yellow—
inconsequential likeness.

Pigment formatted
through light through
lamp through chemical

philanthropy litmus
paper enlargement
"digitally enhanced . . ."

Of yellow ordinarily
optical now chemical
incompatibilities.

STUDIO: LATER THAT DAY

Twin cities: yellow light
Cadmium Yellow Light
emitting voice across skin.

Paper folded to indicate
that Cadmium Yellow Light
and Cadmium Yellow Lemon

are logically off and on
perceptually outbound
culturally orant-splayed.

STUDIO: EARLIER THAT DAY

Twin canvases: red and red
this, meaning regal
that, meaning wedge.

Twin canvases: root and reference
commonplace, revised and reiterated
res and real.

Red and red: see Representation,
see Art History, see Art History:
the Discourse of Representing Red

Yellow and yellow: twin canvases
representing red, meaning regal
increase and immortal coin.

START HERE

Only categorical
value obtains. Yellow.
Analyticity.

Only empty only
value obtains. Yellows
in analyticity. Hello.

[UNTITLED]

mustard
parchment

brilliant yellow
chrome yellow
Naples yellow
yellow ochre

red
yellow
blue

red and yellow and blue by air mail
across from city hall, black and white

red and yellow or blue foliate
mustard and parchment pleat

except for brilliant yellow
chrome yellow without exception

to seem more and more Naples yellow
to make an example of yellow ochre

ON THE NAME OF THE STUDIO

mustard surrenders gradient to straw
parchment lent an attempt at alibi, lemon

Brilliant yellow repudiates the one, as one modern tomorrow laughed
Chrome yellow of the unthought park; some entity today is subsiding
Naples yellow cannot gaze: we, more reminiscent of letting or limiting fiberglass, the
    variable for something positive
Yellow ochre allowing architecture: now one semi-biographical doorsill has "outstripped
    my reading."

A red moon, or its graphical equivalent, requested permission to sustain a lower step.
Here, yellow earth has put an ear to lines and anthems pressed together. See frontispiece.
Set stone. Let us stay a little. Again, the blue sun finds asylum in a plane, plot, in an
    eternity of paper, negative or interrogative.

V.

DELIGHT INSTRUCT

PREFACE THIS

CHORAL TEXT B

The idea for this present study	Impetus	The impetus, presented often anecdotally, emerges as a contingent	avalanche during the Q. and A.
In the course of this study we became convinced	Thesis	The thesis advanced emerges even as research	and its litigants interpret a quite visible diagram.
It is hoped that in the process	Method	The method emerges as advantageous,	slender.
In particular we would like to thank	Acknowledgments	The acknowledgments emerge endowed with and endowing	shadowy lineage: great, greater, greatest.

The preface predicts your text to perfection; the text is left to fend for itself; and/or an index rats on the text.

Preface this with a text predicated on itself: it is perfect; the text enters and is alone; as for the index, it antagonizes the text.

A preface prefers a plan, elevates text through plan and equilibrium; the text veers left; symptomatic are its indices.

Our preface dispenses preliminaries perfectly; the text feeds on conferences and turbulence; we might say that his index defected.

Three groups of hearers: our preface "incorporating the verb *to wish*"; our text in correspondence; your index "alien to the story."

A preface always intrepid in the tropics; a text left to its characteristic predicament; an index of first encounters.

A preface's rights and obligations; a text's singular previously published mechanism; an indexical universe.

INTERIOR

A porch approaches a house, prefaces a house
a porch and its prerequisite format
wrap themselves around the house.
The formula is this: first, house, then, aggrandizement.

First, an anecdotal flurry to visit the onset of writing.
Testifying to unknowing is a first step in the way:
speechlessness in her case, or laughter, as he heard himself;
then, reinstating an anecdote to authenticate the onset of writing.

Causeway between eye and mind he wrote,
because, undoubtedly (later folded, with writing on one side).
The causes of events ever more interesting, rank and overgrown
occasion no boundary yet causes why and wherefore she said he wrote.
(Release from beneath) inferences through reasoning.
That interlacing causes a lace to disappear he would have us say,
with a given event as a starting point, to increase or decrease eclipse
or cure (back and forth and up and down)
or convalescence (mainly by water).

If it is true, to the extent that, theoretically there is nothing to prevent
a fact, at a given moment. How much? The status of
argumentation showing up the remnants.
The rule is, the rule implicit;
by reason of, it is for the reason that;
it should now be clear from, it is clear that what is meant by—
efficient term-with-a-view-to-which brings to pass
manuscripts, especially if one is tempted.
Written dialogue to tempt
combatants: it is a question then. We do not see why.
It is debatable, even if this were feasible. . . .
It is open to question, then. Argumentation by sacrifice:
doing without, the limits to which one will go
to tempt caution. Caution (object A with top view) becomes beautiful if
prolonged (bathing), elongated ("as if for a handle").

CITIES OF THE TABLE

MARGINALIA

1.
Such as we see here
as here and as above, three
echoes are met in encrypted turbulence:
a topic. Contents re-cognizing a list
breaks a very light repose
or not loathsome array of which man takes hold.
Take hold.
"Condensed enumeration" in zeros and ones, apparently

and cantilevering. From the content, the table
of that same content,
we read "Chapter 1" (or more often "1") moving in rented
advantage, much of it; he elsewhere, of what?
As Soon As Possible is content to arrive. And so we subsist on "systematized data"
cantilevering and/or articulating a convoy: 1, 2, at something like full stature.
Advocates place it preceding the text

        "Contents

        Foreword
        Translator's Note
        Architext: an Introduction
        Index"

is an anatomy.

2.
One eye too many?

APPARATUS

Foreword
Introduction
Index
Photographers

and echoes are met in encrypted turbulence:
a topic. Contents re-cognizing a list
breaks a very light repose

where dialectic had been.

List of Plates
Foreword to the First Edition
Foreword to the Second Edition
Foreword to the Pelican Edition
1
2
3
4
5
6
7
Notes
Supplementary Bibliography
Second Supplementary Bibliography
Table of Names and Dates
Index

in zeros and ones, apparently

and cantilevering. From the content, the table
of that same content,

We have reached Chapter 1 (or "1")

Acknowledgments
Notes
Index of First Lines
Index

moving in rented advantage, much of it digestive.

Sampling has distributed the wealth
in corridor throughout acoustic mix, electronic lavatory
through others' interpreted indexical scrapes across the floor of
rhetoric, as here and as here in, of, or not, loathsome.

Of such and such as we see here, here and here: circle and dot are met iterating

a topic, breaking a very light repose above and without.

"Contents

Foreword
Translator's Note
Architext: an Introduction
Index"

Epitome which opens the poetics
discussed ("bracing his left leg against
the border"): Athenian, as advocated.

A shortcut predicted the text. Protocols
crumpled.

Of that same content preceding the
"excitable, degenerate" body we read
rhetoric

where dialectic once was, will have
been scraped of that same content

and imitating the table placed in advance, placed after broad-mouthed Chapter 1.

Of such and such as we see here
here and here: many echoes
are met iterating

a topic. Commentary encrypted within
"pre-existing taxonomies"
etc.

might be better disrobed:

List of Plates
Foreword to the First Edition

Foreword to the Second Edition cantilevering and/or articulating a convoy: 1, 2,

at something like full stature.
Advocates place it preceding the text
Foreword to, a profile preliminary to the main

lyric that amalgamates a schema

Notes
Supplementary Bibliography cantilevering and/or articulating
Second Supplementary Bibliography
Table of Names and Dates, a profile preliminary to the main
Index mediating supplement

might be better to enrobe
grammar
frequently—the known frequency

being a sign. A sign
foraging within an appendix
might be spent

in necessity, he said
wrote twice.

Signature

1.

The pen is on the table.

Cantilevering from the content, the table

Advocates place it antecedently, alternatively throughout

his constantly recurring body more or less textual.

We are at table.

Tables: placement of, in manuscript.

No "light table" appears in this edition

obedient to "light pen" still.

"To remove from consideration indefinitely"

is not the same as "having a plane surface."

The light pen rests satisfactorily

on the incised folding table, upon the unruly fold-out table.

2.

The winged pen rests.

Cantilevering from the content, the other larger slab.

Accompanied by a dog or standing apart,

he hears it also.

We are at table.

Chronological tables, with rustic setting.

"Light tables," "light pen"—few and far between are these phrases

in reference to advancing light traveling a light-year.

"Condensed enumeration"

"Systematized data"

with text to follow in imitation, promoted.

Protocols, stationed beneath handles.

All falling pens, some stationary tables.
Cantilevering from the content, Contents
  Contents
  Chapter 1 . . .
Advocates place it in advance; proponents sum up
the body, the body dolorous and difficult.

"Light tables" are fast, faster; "light tables" becoming obsolete
"The Auroras of Autumn" may well have had life
  in hallucinatory aftermath: see "light shows"
  Contents
  Chapter 1 . . .
The light pens rest satisfactorily archaic,
electric, acoustic, electronic—in kaleidoscopic life-blood.

                                  We read
an injured translator's note, an apologetic translation
an apodictic profile throughout the body

As Soon As Possible is Fragile Contents. Priority,
with text. This codicil should be spent within the text.

A list burrowing into a signature, a list cantilevering
syllabus within "pre-existing taxonomies" etc.

At issue is a table to stand upon. At issue is a table
imitating the grammar of that same folding table,

of that same focal point. The preface may say—indeed does.
"Even as I write these words," the author may never have said.

Saying as though through earlier versions, and to what and to whom
we owe this work-in-progress, is author-as-stutterer. To whom

is the index speaking? To what? What the text actually said, as against what claim
preliminary to sense, may be an index, an index "which seems to me to beckon"

value by the chapter. Sputter ruminative minutes concerning obsolete sentences,
then limit sense and worry a length of compendious something.

Axiom, carry out atmosphere!
Epitome Stunned Immortal Source Text!

"A sign foisted off on the appendix" tempting text that might think,
he said, he wrote, quoting a deferred bandwidth and literature.

HEREAFTER

1.

The End.

In an earlier version of this paper, in earliest delight or design

please find superfluity, an endnote described as notched and proliferating

rhetoric of extra identity, extra to the far-flung bed, across it and throughout—

we have seen enough bed in earlier versions. To put it another way:

of failure to mean and/or to have meant and/or to emend, now described as notched and

proliferating silverplate, is a more sympathetic reading, a smothering reading.

The End.

By the side of the road, alternative versions of this erasure.

Enough erasure found—in endnotes! we say

to ourselves and to someone else. Memoranda formatted as "color commentary"

becomes your ha-ha, a sunk fence. Whenever historians speak of themselves,

(we say to ourselves and to someone else), when historians erupt,

whenever historians forget the equivalent of a manuscript, they add its equivalent in a

venting hole.

Arising from the attempt, a prototype left in the variables. Acquisitions. A sizable literature

has grown up around a wealth of erasure. Item: A rubbing.

The End.

End the immunity, fall prey to hair

and string, for we follow the thread of a more sympathetic, less sympathetic speculative reach

subjecting repleteness to intestine, beneath and apart yet curiously animated.

For a less sympathetic account, see "hairsplitting."

2.

A draft. Alternative take: take
and/or drift in footnotes, we decant notes to the foot beneath,
beneath the perforated line,
to start coagulating, congratulating itself, to start accusing itself. We reject
text as intrinsic in favor of text replete with interconnectedness.

A draft:
evidence of the experimental math: translator's footnote
cites method restored to misanthropy in you, writer,
becoming negativity on the frontiers
of the sieve, dented yet replete.
A narrative: David appears.

A draft
and/or our descant of second guessing, which is visible
content beyond the scope of, etc., for drawing inferences. Further research suggested.
Also second guessing consigned to congratulating itself. Draft *fort . . . da*
where such ramified approaches would burden the text proper. Immodesty welcome.

Draft
and/or decant foot.

DELIGHT INSTRUCT

1.

With expectations prepared to be inventing
the text of that half-open book, that book there, we are selectively it.
It? An index sewn

to abstract nouns.

Of interesting silk appropriated, prepared to be firmament

on a two-inch string
The blue sea on a two-inch string
The blue sea on a two-inch string only proves the rule.

Index intercepting text
a text throughout index, whenever an index in abstract
an index in concrete

correlates to text not to tile . . . title.

Of nouns tethered to spine.

Of difference throughout index measuring the text in attendance.

2.

The reader leapt through the index
To save time

the reader leapt through the scrim.

This is a test, a breakthrough for readers in reading rooms.
They have leapt through many Kraft paper screens

have broke through colloquially—a hiatus!

3.

The index accommodated curvature
through proper names.
Commence to count the lines assigned to Freud's rival: therein lies

subjectivity whistling

Commence to read the index of this book, of that, to compare
lines assigned to Freud's rival, and so to ascertain
oasis therein.

Sum and substance whistling through the walls

A field near a far farmhouse assigned to Freud's rival
has come to inflame the index
and take the initiative:

who is whistling?

A hiatus in the hunt, a field near a farmhouse
inflecting the index assigned to Freud's rival
perspectives

whistling is its own infield.

4.

Consisting primarily of an itemized list
hand-in-hand with immobility studding the top.
Hand-in-hand immobility
Hand-in-hand immobility in and of
Hand-in-hand immobility in and of synchrony, primarily.
Yes. Immediacy.
Much gratified by neurons firing (yours).
Much gratified by neurons firing. Yours sincerely, . . .
Such are the diverging extremes,
the diverging of "Yours sincerely," from "(yours)" in the above.

5.

Yes, as abiding content and spirit in the following feast: "Hi! No!"
Displaying what he knows since, with "Hi! No! Hi! No! arising from this project,
non-negatively. Next is a discussion,
mostly living, and with largely lurid details: "PpulrpNleK" and sound poetry.
"Poetry is a mental event—Thwack!" "Next!" The new rhetoric
looks at the arts. "Hi! No! Thwack! I acquit!"

Mostly living and with largely lurid details is "Hi! No!" in the affirmative
greeting from the infant's displaying what he, the umpire, does—the requisite
rhetoric for abiding content and spirit. "Hi! No! A mental event—thwack! Next. New!"
The new rhetoric in the clutch of the waltz, the waltz instructed by the march,
struck, and sound poetry. "Poetry is a mental event—Thwack!" That, his promise
acting under duress and remaining *Symphony No. 6* throughout, struck the aptness.

"Out! Yes! Hi! No!" like a promise stuck
in diaspora greeting the infant. With largely lurid details and "Next!"
mostly living a mental event aggravated with imperatives
that is his format, the infant greets the adult. "PpurlpNleK"
in graphic description has captivated the waltz,
with a taste not unlike sandpaper across woodblocks.

6.

index text registers thesis this unconfessed register magisterial belief
index indent indebted to reading relative incurrence

To submit the officiating text to a test of its unconfessed register, first read the index.
In a first reading through its index, the charismatic text is tested.
To ascertain authoritative texts informing this
belief by informing that indent (incurrence),
slip into theoretical studies of the thesis hidden in the index;
the index confesses to scarifications unconfessed in the body of the text.
Our reading the index to reveal the simultaneity prior to the text
will make descent into priority—agriculture, cattle raising—
for the index values the sense actually manifest that the magisterial title cries out.
Expectations are not lost upon the title: the title boasts, is delighted and indecent.
The index punctures the equanimity of the text at long last:
the testing of the text, the torment issuing from
nominative belief informing that indent (incurrence)
enumerating names, and through the definite spatial plan of the deceased
we postulate authoritative texts, possess the paradigm, the false door.

7.

Like a window not immediately obvious.
Sense, the inexpressive mention.
For which footfall?
He is hard on narrative.

8.
If Flaubert is innumerable, or, else, if "Flaubert" is numerous
and if "Flaubert" along with "Forster" is more numerous than "Freud," then
erasure becoming a must is an elemental gauntlet proper to nouns.

Without the nouns, without nouns equaling ideas, an index of nothing but "Flaubert"
is notable; with he more numerous in name than "Freud " in this case, so literature or literary
crescendo can be said, is said to be designated

of a code. If "Fielding," "Flaubert" and "Forster" eagerly await the literary
matter probabilistic, with its ups and downs, then gathering etiquette
to themselves are these proper names in particularity

only, saving ancient space. In a box
of abandoned enterprise without universals, a name weighs
some number: what does it mean in daylight, the volume so deleted of topics,

it saves space by remaining empty: this is a test or a deck of despotism
or a token. Enumeration gives vehement weight to celebrity. Count the mentions,
the various attempts at mention, the revenge of more minerals

written there. "Thenceforward it proliferated." Oval in section, the signature frequenting
    the index.
Frequency of something is an index to vehement weight: the rhetoric yclept cliff,
cliff entitled there on the various attempts to exile an index to the back of everything

alphabetically, distributively. The index distributes its sources, specifically, gathering
    etiquette gathering
affiliation, the fringe of which you read as theory of the literary index becoming a must,
an ought, in mathematizing creases from a number that appears to refer to a page.

". . . Cézanne who spent who spent afternoons . . .": that, an author's implicit criteria
through who goes furthest in mention against the glass to accrue subentries (F's rival, etc.).
    If names retire,
name the criteria once frequenting the index. A kind of forensics of situations is under way.

FUNDER ACKNOWLEDGMENTS

Coffee House Press is an independent nonprofit literary publisher. Our books are made possible through the generous support of grants and gifts from many foundations, corporate giving programs, individuals, and through state and federal support. This project received major funding from the National Endowment for the Arts, a federal agency. Coffee House Press has also received support from the Minnesota State Arts Board, through an appropriation by the Minnesota State Legislature and by the National Endowment for the Arts; and from the Elmer and Eleanor Andersen Foundation; the Buuck Family Foundation; the Bush Foundation; the Grotto Foundation; the Lerner Family Foundation; the McKnight Foundation; the Outagamie Foundation; the John and Beverly Rollwagen Foundation; the law firm of Schwegman, Lundberg, Woessner & Kluth, P.A.; Target, Marshall Field's, and Mervyn's with support from the Target Foundation; James R. Thorpe Foundation; West Group; the Woessner Freeman Foundation; and many individual donors.

This activity is made possible in part by a grant from the Minnesota State Arts Board, through an appropriation by the Minnesota State Legislature and a grant from the National Endowment for the Arts.

MINNESOTA
STATE ARTS BOARD

NATIONAL
ENDOWMENT
FOR THE ARTS

To you and our many readers across the country,
we send our thanks for your continuing support.

Good books are brewing at coffeehousepress.org

OTHER TITLES OF INTEREST FROM COFFEE HOUSE PRESS

Available at fine bookstores everywhere.
Good books are brewing at coffeehousepress.org.

Coffee House Press is a nonprofit literary publisher
supported in part by the generosity of readers like you.
We hope the spirit of our books makes you seek out
and enjoy additional titles on our list.
For information on how you can help bring great literature
onto the page, visit coffeehousepress.org.